'Twas the
Night Before
Christmas

Illustrated by John Joven

'Twas the night before Christmas, when all through the house,
Not a creature was stirring, not even a mouse.
The stockings were hung by the chimney with care,
In hopes that St. Nicholas soon would be there.
The children were nestled all snug in their beds,
While visions of sugar plums danced in their heads.

And Mama in her 'kerchief, and I in my cap,

Had just settled our brains for a long winter's nap.

When out on the lawn there arose such a clatter,

I sprang from the bed to see what was the matter.

Away to the window I flew like a flash,
Tore open the shutters and threw up the sash.

The moon on the breast of the new-fallen snow
Gave the lustre of mid-day to objects below.
When, what to my wondering eyes should appear,
But a miniature sleigh, and eight tiny reindeer.

With a little old driver, so lively and quick,
I knew in a moment it must be St. Nick.
More rapid than eagles his coursers they came,
And he whistled, and shouted,
and called them by name:

"Now Dasher! Now, Dancer! Now, Prancer and Vixen!
On, Comet! On, Cupid! On Donder and Blitzen!

To the top of the porch! To the top of the wall!
Now dash away! Dash away! Dash away all!"

As dry leaves that before the wild hurricane fly,
When they meet with an obstacle, mount to the sky.
So up to the house-top the coursers they flew,
With the sleigh full of toys, and St. Nicholas too.

And then, in a twinkling, I heard on the roof
The prancing and pawing of each little hoof.

As I drew in my head, and was turning around,
Down the chimney St. Nicholas came with a bound.
He was dressed all in fur, from his head to his foot,
And his clothes were all tarnished with ashes and soot.

A bundle of toys he had flung on his back,
And he looked like a peddler just opening his pack.

His eyes – how they twinkled! His dimples how merry!

His cheeks were like roses, his nose like a cherry!

His droll little mouth was drawn up like a bow

And the beard of his chin was as white as the snow.

The stump of a pipe he held tight in his teeth,
And the smoke it encircled his head like a wreath.
He had a broad face and a little round belly,
That shook when he laughed, like a bowlful of jelly.

He was chubby and plump, a right jolly old elf,
And I laughed when I saw him, in spite of myself.
A wink of his eye and a twist of his head,
Soon gave me to know I had nothing to dread.

He spoke not a word, but went straight to his work,
And filled all the stockings, then turned with a jerk.

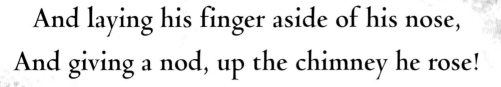

And laying his finger aside of his nose,
And giving a nod, up the chimney he rose!

He sprang to his sleigh, to his team gave a whistle,
And away they all flew like the down of a thistle.
But I heard him exclaim, 'ere he drove out of sight,

"Happy Christmas to all, and to all a good night!"

About the poem

'Twas the Night Before Christmas first appeared anonymously in the New York *Troy Sentinel* newspaper. It was published in December 1823, under the title *Account of a Visit from St. Nicholas.* Several years later, a New York professor named Clement Clarke Moore said he had written it — but some people believe it was written by another New Yorker, Henry Livingston Jr.

Music composed and produced by Anthony Marks
Designed by Caroline Spatz   Edited by Lesley Sims
Digital manipulation: Nick Wakeford

This edition first published in 2013 by Usborne Publishing Ltd., Usborne House, 83-85 Saffron Hill, London EC1N 8RT, England.
www.usborne.com Copyright © 2013, 2011 Usborne Publishing Ltd.